Bunnies & Blossoms

by
Eleanor Burns

Third Edition
Copyright © 1991 by Eleanor Burns

to Orion - A Five - Year - Old Expert Bunny Maker
The whole Bunnysock Family sleeps with him;

to Grant - A Baseball Superstar
The baseball glove tooth fairy pillow is just for him.

Love, Mom 1980

Third Edition
First Printing - April, 1991
© 1991 by Eleanor Burns

Second Edition
First Printing - January, 1980
© 1981 by Eleanor Burns

First Edition
First Printing - March, 1980
© 1980 by Eleanor Burns

Text design - Pam Nedlic, Graphic Communications.

Cover design and Illustrations - Quilt in a Day Graphics

Contents

1. The Bunny Socks Family

Bunny Socks Family Materials:
Plain white cotton socks.
Baby Bunny - infant sock
Brother and Sister - child's sock
Father and Mother - adult sock

Tail - white *pompom* cut from ball fringe
Teeth - piece of white felt
Eyes - 2 black shank buttons
Nose - 1 skein of pink embroidery floss
Whiskers - 1 skein black embroidery floss or black carpet thread
White thread and needle
Polyester fiberfill

sock - bunny
toes - ears
heel - face
ankle - body

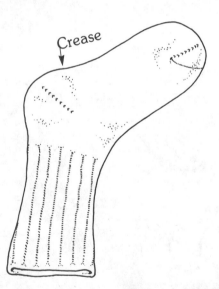

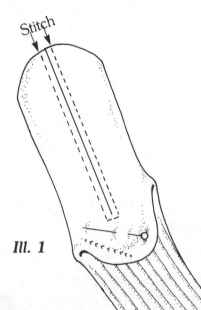

Ill. 1

1. **Ears:** Turn the sock wrong side out. Fold so that the crease falls down the middle of the sock toward the heel. *Ill. 1*
2. Place a pin just above the heel to divide the *face* from the *ears*.
3. Machine stitch or hand stitch down the toes to the pin, pivot, and stitch back up. Use the crease as a guide.
4. Cut between the ears, following the crease line.

5. Turn right side out.
6. With a long double strand of thread and needle, gather each ear tightly at the base. Wrap the ear bases and stitch from front to back several times for durability. The ears flop down the back. *(Do not cut the thread. This needle will be used to sew on the eyes and teeth.)* **Ill. 2**
7. Stuff the head and body with fiberfill. The heel sticks out and forms the face.
8. With the second needle, sew the bottom shut by overlapping and stitching.
9. Pinch in a triangular indentation for the two eyes and the teeth below the nose. **Ill. 3**
10. With the thread hanging from the ears, stitch through the fiberfill back and forth between the eyes and teeth, pulling tightly to give indentations.

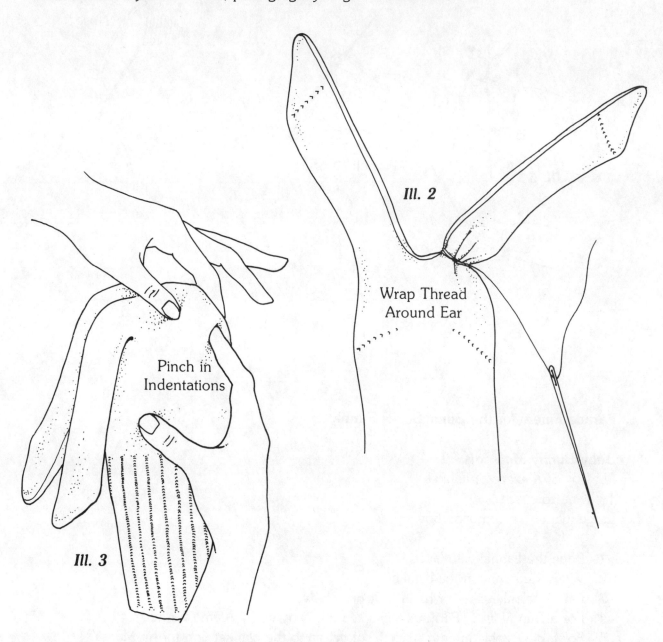

Ill. 2

Wrap Thread
Around Ear

Pinch in
Indentations

Ill. 3

11. Stitch the triangular indentation again, sewing on the shank button eyes and white felt teeth.
12. With the pink embroidery floss, *satin stitch* a triangular shaped nose. Draw the floss from behind the teeth so the knot is invisible. ***Ill. 4***
13. Stitch french knots on each side of the nose for whiskers or draw long strands of carpet thread through for hanging whiskers. ***Ill. 5***
14. With a long, double strand of thread and needle, sew on the pompom tail.
15. Draw the thread through the fiberfill to the *belly button*, pull tight and stitch back to the tail. Knot the thread and cut.

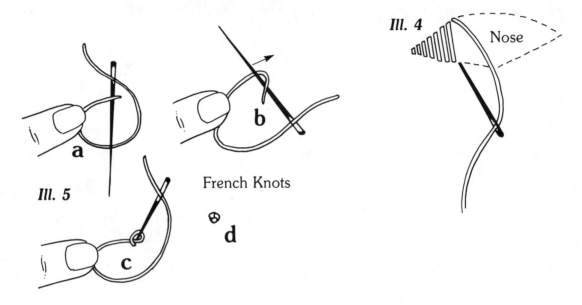

Ill. 4 — Nose

Ill. 5 — a, b, c, d — French Knots

Parade Finery for the BunnySocks Family

Baby Bunny Materials:
8½" × 8½" piece of flannel
1 yd. narrow lace
Large diaper pin or ribbon bow

1. Edge the flannel with lace.
2. Wrap the bunny in the blanket.
3. Pin the blanket shut or hand tack on a bow.
4. For a Bunny Hug: Permanently stitch the baby in the Mama's arms.
5. For a detachable bunny, stitch 1" of velcro to the blanket and to the Mama's arms.

Brother and Sister Bunny Materials:

Shirt - 6" × 20" piece of T-shirt knit fabric

Hands - 2 pompoms cut from ball fringe

Girl Bunny - ½ yd. lace

Handfull of fiberfill

Carrot - scraps of orange and green felt

1. Cut the shirt front and back on the fold.
2. **Boy's shirt:** Turn under ¼" at the neck and bottom. Stitch. ***Ill. 6***
   Girl's shirt: Trim the neck and hem with lace. ***Ill. 7***
3. With right sides together, stitch the side arm seams.
4. Slip the shirt on the bunny from the bottom.
5. Handstitch the shirt on securely around the neck.
6. Stuff the sleeves with fiberfill.
7. Sew *pompom* hands on the ends.

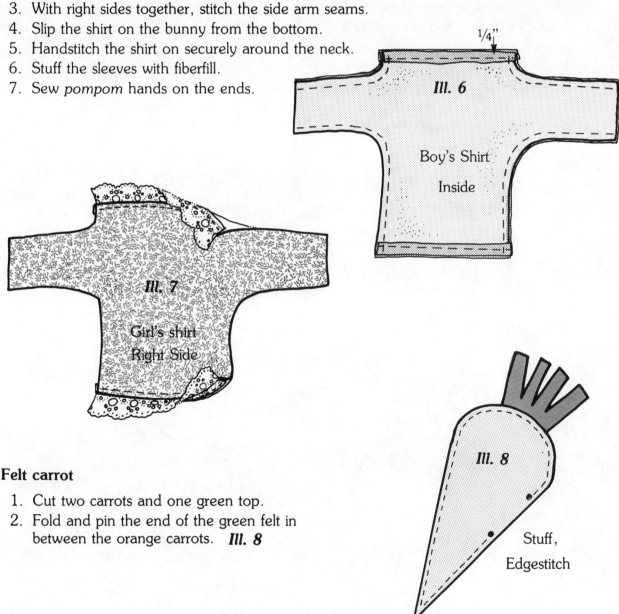

Felt carrot

1. Cut two carrots and one green top.
2. Fold and pin the end of the green felt in between the orange carrots. ***Ill. 8***

3. Stitch around the outside edge, stuffing lightly before completing the seam.
4. Handtack the carrot in the child's arms.

Mama Bunny Materials:

Dress - ⅓ yd. calico

Lace and ribbon - assortment of 20" pieces

Hands - 2 pompoms cut from ball fringe

Apron and hat - 1 piece of felt

2 buttons

2 small artificial flowers

Hat - 14" rickrack

1. **Mother's Dress:** Cut two on the fold.
2. With right sides together, stitch the dress above one sleeve.
3. Trim the neckline and the cuff with lace.
4. Stitch the underarm.
5. Trim the hemline with assorted laces.
6. Complete the opposite side in the same manner.
7. Slip the dress on the Mama from the bottom. With hand stitching, gather and pull the dress tight to fit the neck.
8. Hand tack on a bow.
9. Stuff the sleeves with fiberfill.
10. Gather the ends of the sleeves and sew on *pompom* hands.

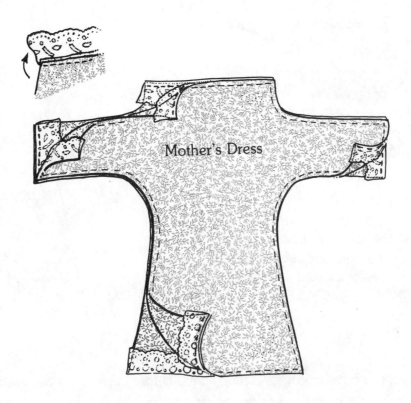

11. **Mother's Apron:** Cut 1 from felt on the fold.
12. Sew on lace around the outside edge.
13. Criss cross the straps in the back of Mama.
14. Sew the straps in place with buttons.
15. **Mother's Hat:** Cut one hat from felt.
16. Sew rickrack or lace trim around the edge of the brim.
17. Machine tack on the artificial flowers.
18. Fold right sides together, matching notches on the center back. Stitch ¼" seam. *Ill. 1*
19. Refold and stitch ¼" seam. *Ill. 2*
20. Cut slits for bunny ears. Draw the ears of the bunny through.

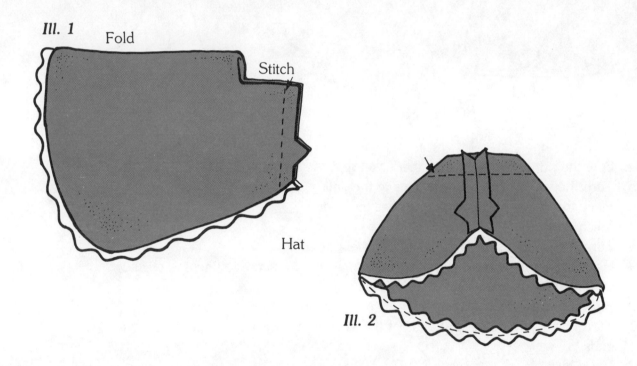

Ill. 1 Fold Stitch Hat *Ill. 2*

Papa Bunny Materials:
Jacket - ¼ yd. corduroy
Lining - 16" × 7" piece of fabric
2 buttons
Miniature straw hat (available at craft shops)
Miniature straw basket (available at craft shops)

1. Cut 1 jacket back and 1 lining back on the fold, 2 jacket fronts and 2 front linings, and 2 sleeves. (The sleeves are not lined.)

2. Sew the shoulder seams on the jacket and on the lining. *Ill. 3*
3. Lay the jacket flat. Place the sleeves right sides together to the jacket. Stitch around the top of the sleeve. *Ill. 4*

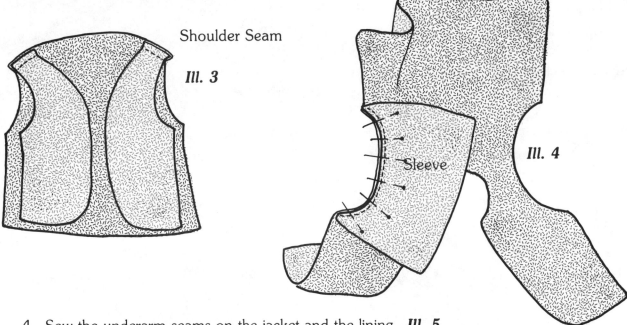

Shoulder Seam

Ill. 3

Ill. 4

Sleeve

4. Sew the underarm seams on the jacket and the lining. *Ill. 5*
5. Turn the jacket right side out. Leave the lining inside out.
6. Place the jacket and lining right sides together.
7. Stitch around the outside edge. *Ill. 6*
8. Turn the jacket through the lining armhole opening.
9. Wrap the jacket around the papa bunny. Sew it in place by stitching on the buttons through the jacket and the sock.
10. Stuff the sleeves with fiberfill.
11. Turn under and gather the ends of the sleeves. Sew *pompom* hands on the ends.
12. Hand tack a basket in his arms. Place a straw hat on his head.

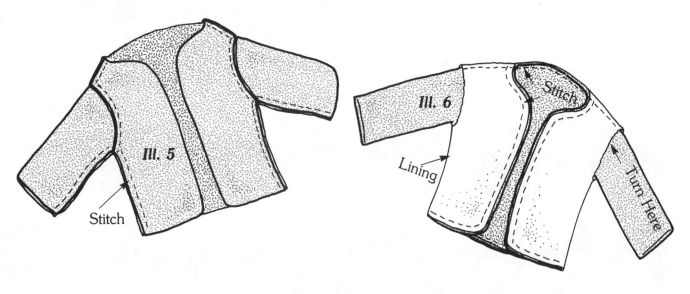

Ill. 5

Stitch

Ill. 6

Lining

Stitch

Turn Here

2. Soft Basket

Soft Basket Materials:
Basket - ½ yd. calico
Lining - ½ yd. calico
⅛ yd. stiff bonded batting
½ yd. polyester fleece
½ yd. heavy iron-on interfacing
2 yds. string or crochet thread
1 yd. eyelet lace trim

1. **Basket:** Cut 1 basket, 1 basket lining, 1 iron-on interfacing, and 1 polyester fleece basket. Iron on the interfacing to the wrong side of the calico basket.
2. Pin the polyester fleece to the wrong side of the calico lining. Fold right sides together matching numbers. Sew a ¼" seam on all 4 sides of the calico basket **Ill. 1** and lining. **Ill. 2**

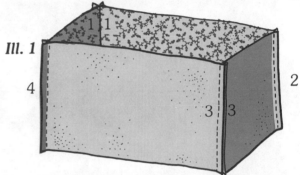

Ill. 1

Ill. 2

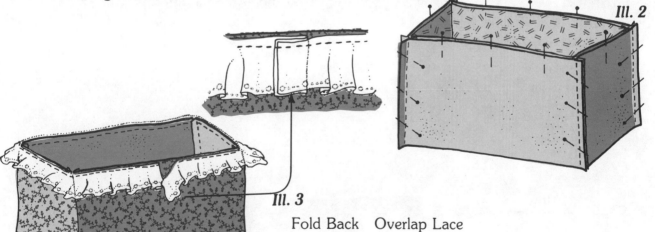

Ill. 3

Fold Back   Overlap Lace

3. Fold the basket right side out. Leave the lining wrong side out.
4. Fold back 1" of the eyelet trim. With right sides together, stitch the trim around the top of the basket. Overlap the last 1" of eyelet and cut off the excess. *Ill. 3*
5. Turn the eyelet to stand up. Tuck the raw seam allowance inside.

6. Press the top edge of the lining under ¼" toward the wrong side.

7. Set the lining inside the basket. Pin the lining in place so that the folded top edge of the lining is 1/8" higher than the line of stitching on the eyelet.

8. From the right side, *stitch in the ditch* where the eyelet meets the basket. Do not stitch the two sections allowed for the braided handle insert. **Ill. 4**

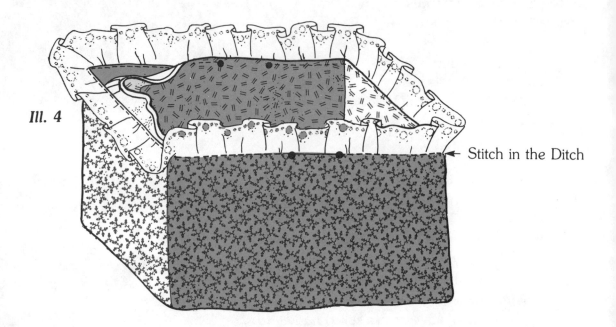

Ill. 4

← Stitch in the Ditch

1. **Braided Handle:** Cut 3 - 18" x 2 ¼"strips of calico and iron-on interfacing. Cut 2 strips from the basket fabric and 1 from the lining fabric. Iron on the interfacing to the wrong side of the calico. Cut 3–18" x ¾" strips of fleece.

2. Fold the calico strips right sides together lengthwise.

3. *Speed Sew Method* of turning: Lay the string along the fold line in the interior of the strip.   Insert ½" of the fleece into the middle of the strip.

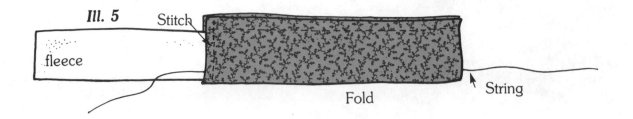

Ill. 5   Stitch

fleece

Fold

String

4. Stitch back and forth across the string several times at one end. Stitch one long side with a ¼" seam. **Ill. 5**

5. Tug lightly on the string and pull the calico tube right side out. *Ill. 6*
6. Cut off the string and stitching at the narrow end. Pull the string out.

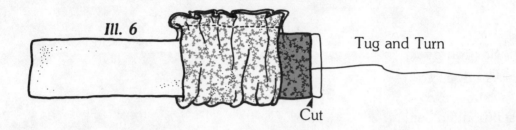

Ill. 6   Tug and Turn

Cut

7. Stitch all 3 calico tubes together at one end. Braid. Stitch the opposite end.
8. Insert the braided handle into the two open places on the basket and stitch in place.

1. **Soft Fabric Bow:** Cut 2 pieces 5" × 11" from the lining fabric.
2. Fold 1 crosswise and 1 lengthwise, right sides together.
3. Cut the batting the same sizes as the 2 folded pieces.
4. Pin the batting to the backs of the 2 folded pieces.
5. Stitch a ¼" seam, following the diagram. *Ill. 7*
6. Turn the pieces through the holes in the centers.
7. Hand pleat the pieces through the centers and pin.
8. Fold the long piece over the top of the rectangle.
9. Stitch through all thicknesses. *Ill. 8*
10. Hand stitch the bow to the basket.

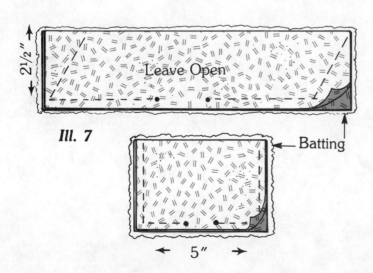

2½"

Leave Open

Batting

Ill. 7

5"

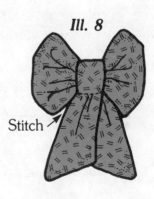

Ill. 8

Stitch

3. Jewelry Box

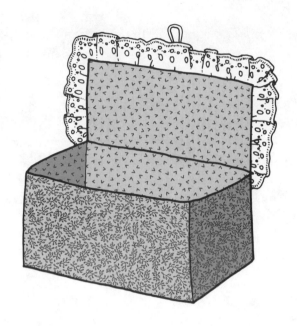

Jewelry Box Materials:

Basket - ½ yd. calico
Lining - ½ yd. calico
⅛ yd. stiff bonded batting
1 yd. eyelet lace trim
1-22" piece of ribbon
½ yd. iron-on interfacing
½ yd. polyester fleece

1. **Box:** Follow the directions in steps 1, 2, and 3 for the soft basket.
2. Put the lining inside the basket matching seams. Sew around the top edge leaving a 3" opening in the back for turning. Turn the basket right side out. Slipstitch the opening shut. *Ill. 1*
3. **Lid:** Cut 2 pieces calico, one iron-on interfacing, and one polyester fleece. Iron on the interfacing to the wrong side of 1 calico lid.
4. Fold back 1" of the eyelet trim. With right sides of the eyelet and the basket calico together, pin the trim around the edge of the lid. Overlap the last 1" of eyelet and cut off the excess. Pin the 2 pieces of calico right sides together, with the fleece on the bottom. *Ill. 3*

Lining   *Ill. 1*

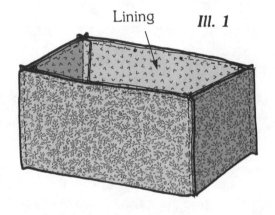

Ill. 2

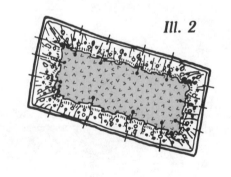
Ill. 2

Ill. 3

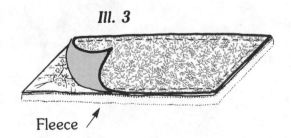

Fleece

5. Sew around the outside edge, leaving a 4" opening for turning.
6. Turn. Slipstitch the opening shut.
7. Pin the lid in place.
8. Lay the box and lid flat, lining sides together. *Stitch in the ditch* through the eyelet, lid and box. ***Ill. 4***
9. **Ribbon Clasp:** Cut the ribbon into 6" and 16" pieces.
10. Make a loop out of the 6" piece. Pin it in the center front of the lid.
11. Lay the 16" piece across it. Stitch through all thicknesses. Tie the 16" piece into a bow. ***Ill. 5***

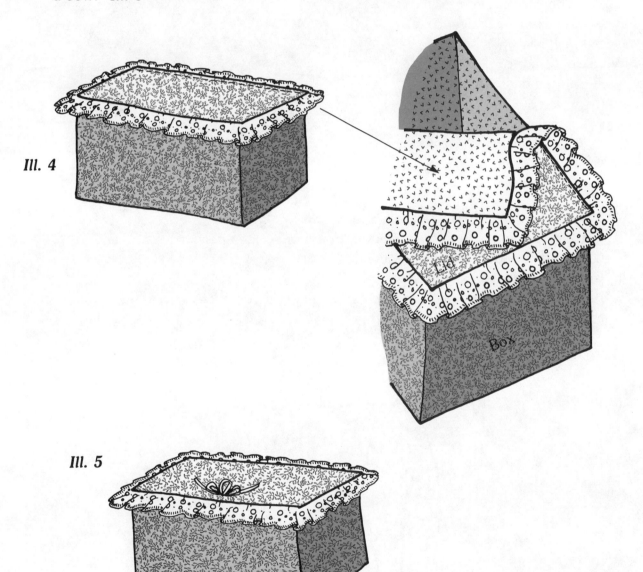

Ill. 4

Ill. 5

4. Bunny Ball

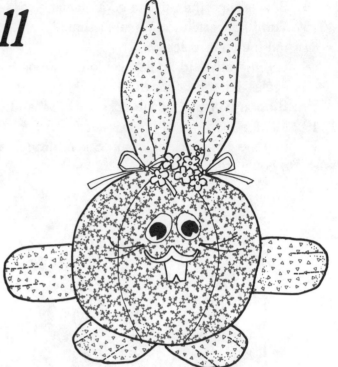

Bunny Ball Materials:

Body - ⅓ yd. calico
Ears, Arms, Feet - ¼ yd. contrasting calico
Tail - 1 *pompom* cut from ball fringe
Eyes - black or blue and white felt
Nose - pink felt
Whiskers - 1 yd. carpet thread
⅛ yd. stiff bonded batting
1 - 16" piece of ribbon
1 small artificial flower
7" × 7" piece of heavy iron-on interfacing
½ lb. fiberfill stuffing
1 miniature basket

1. Cut 6 bodies and 2 pairs each of the ears, hands, and feet.
2. Cut 2 ears from the iron-on interfacing. Iron it on to the wrong side of 2 ears.
3. Cut 2 hands and 2 feet from the bonded batting.
4. Cut out the felt facial features.
5. **Ears:** With right sides together, stitch around the outside edge, leaving the bottom open.

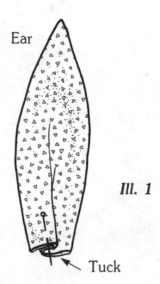

Ear

Ill. 1

Tuck

6. Turn and press. Pin in a small tuck. Pin in place on the center back section of the body.   *Ill. 1*
7. Stitch or glue the felt facial features into place on the center front section.

8. Sew 3 body sections together to make 2 halves. *The ears are in the center of the back body section. The face is in the center of the front body section.* **Speed Sew Method:** *Ill. 2 Ill. 3*

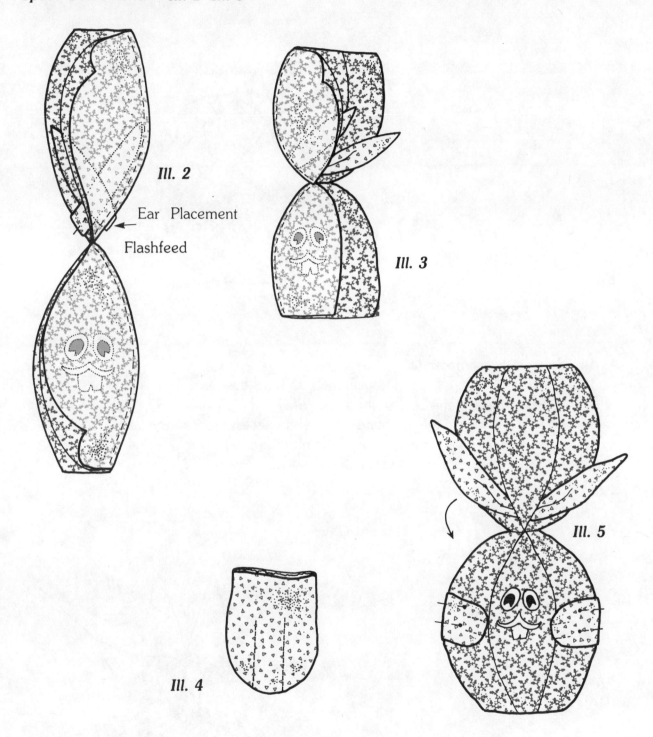

Ill. 2

Ear Placement

Flashfeed

Ill. 3

Ill. 5

Ill. 4

9. **Hands and Feet:** With right sides together, stitch around the outside edge. Turn. Stuff lightly with bonded batting. Topstitch on the dashed lines. *Ill. 4*
10. Pin the hands in place on both sides of the front half of the body.
11. Put the two body halves right sides together and stitch around the outside edge. *Ill. 5*

12. Turn right side out through the hole in the bottom, and stuff with fiberfill.
13. Overlap the feet on the bottom of the body and stitch in place, covering the opening at the same time. ***Ill. 6***

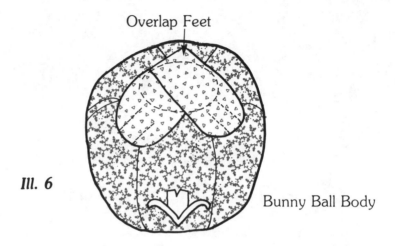

Overlap Feet

Ill. 6

Bunny Ball Body

14. Sew on the *pompom* tail.
15. Stand the ears up and tack together 2" up from the base. Tack a bow and an artificial flower at the base of the ears. ***Ill. 7***
16. Wrap the arm through the handle on the basket and tack to the body.
17. Stitch french knots on each side of the mouth for whiskers or draw long strands of carpet thread through for hanging whiskers.

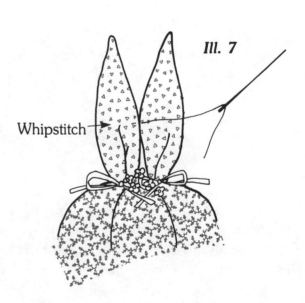

Ill. 7

Whipstitch

5. Calico Roses

Calico Roses Materials:

3 assorted pieces of calico 4" × 5" (1 piece for each rose)
Artificial rose leaves (found in craft shops)
Green floral tape (found in craft shops)
Round wooden toothpicks
Sprig of dried baby's breath
1-16" piece of ribbon

1. Cut 3 pieces of fabric 4" × 5".
2. Fold right sides together, and sew a ¼" seam along the 5" side to form a tube.
   Speed Sew Method: see illustration **1 Ill.**

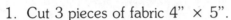

5"

2"

1 Ill.   Snip   Snip

3. Turn right side out.
4. Insert about 1" of the toothpick inside one end of the tube.
5. Gather the fabric around the toothpick, and hold a rose leaf along side the gathered fabric. **2 Ill.**
6. Tightly wrap the gathered fabric and rose leaf with green floral tape.
7. Puff the rose out with your fingers and fold the top of the fabric tube to the inside to form a rosebud. **3 Ill.**
8. Wrap the three roses and baby's breath with floral tape. Tie with a ribbon.

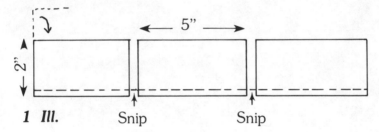

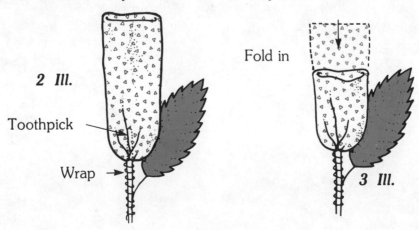

2 Ill.

Toothpick

Wrap →

Fold in

3 Ill.

6. Potpourri Eggs

Potpourri Egg Materials:

Assorted pieces of calico approximately 7" × 12" each

Assorted pieces of lace, rickrack, and trim

Potpourri or dried rose petals.

1. Cut out several pairs of eggs.
2. On the top, right side of the egg, sew on the trim. **Speed Sew Method:** *Do not cut the lace to the size of one egg. Sew the lace on several eggs at a time by butting the eggs after each other. Cut between the eggs.* **Ill. 1**

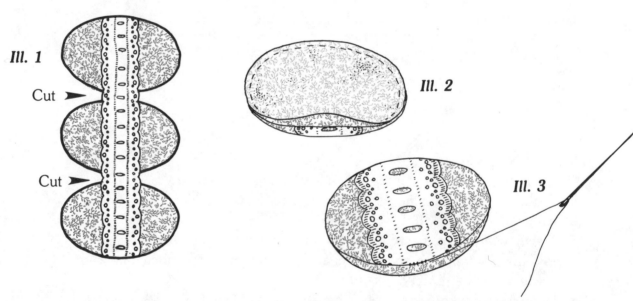

Ill. 1

Cut ▶

Cut ▶

Ill. 2

Ill. 3

3. Pin the decorated front and the plain back right sides together. **Ill. 2**
4. Stitch around the outside edge with a ¼" seam allowance, leaving an opening for turning.
5. Turn.
6. Stuff lightly with potpourri.
7. Slipstitch the opening shut. **Ill. 3**

7. Sunbonnets for Children

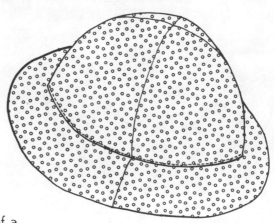

Sunbonnets for Children Materials:

Girl's Hat
¼ yd. heavy fabric
¼ yd. iron-on interfacing
2-18" pieces of ribbon for ties
1 yd. rickrack for trim on brim
                    OR
1 yd. pre-gathered eyelet lace used in place of a brim

Boy's Hat
¼ yd. heavy fabric
¼ yd. iron-on interfacing
1 yd. bias tape

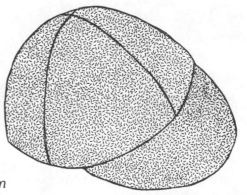

20" Head size for children under 3 — Use ½" seam allowance.
22" Head size for children over 3 — Use ¼" seam allowance.

Speed Sew Method:

Boy's and Girl's crown: (Iron on interfacing to 4 crown pieces.)
1. Cut 4 crown pieces. With right sides together, and top points touching, stitch 2 pairs of crown pieces together. ***Ill. 1***
2. Match 2 sections right sides together, and stitch. ***Ill. 2***
3. Turn right side out.

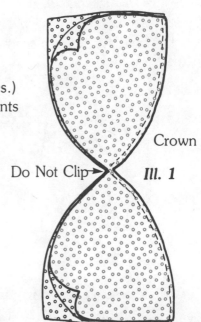

Crown

Do Not Clip➤   ***Ill. 1***

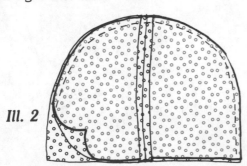

Ill. 2

Girl's Fabric Brim:

1. Cut 4 on the fold from the heavy fabric. Cut 2 on the fold from the iron-on interfacing.
2. Iron on the interfacing to the wrong sides of 2 of the pieces.
3. With right sides together, stitch 2 sets of the brim pieces together to make 2 circles. *Ill. 3*

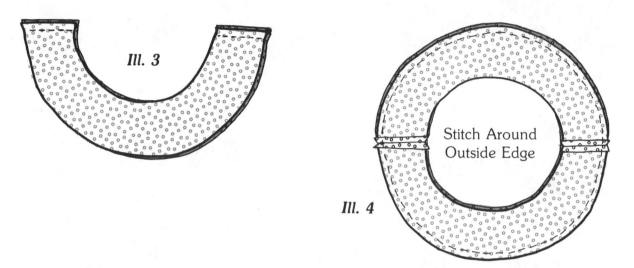

Ill. 3

Stitch Around
Outside Edge

Ill. 4

4. With the right sides of the circles together and the seams matched, stitch around the outside edge. *Ill. 4*
5. Turn and press.
6. With right sides together, match the notches and seams on the brim to the seams on the hat.
7. Stretch and pin the brim to the hat. Stitch. Finish the inside raw edge with a zigzag stitch. *Ill. 5*
8. Decorate the brim with rows of topstitching or rickrack.
9. Tack the ties in place on the inside of the hat where the crown meets the brim.

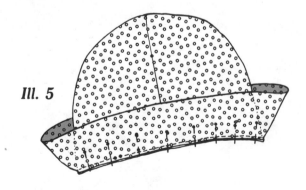

Ill. 5

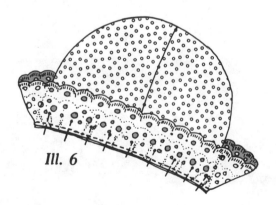

Ill. 6

Girl's Eyelet Lace Brim: *Ill. 6*

1. Stitch the pre-gathered eyelet lace to the crown.

22

Boy's Visor:

1. Cut 2 from heavy fabric. Cut 1 from iron-on interfacing.
2. Iron on the interfacing to the wrong side of one of the visor pieces.
3. With the two pieces right sides together, stitch around the outside edge. **Ill. 1**
4. Turn and press. Topstitch the outside edge. **Ill. 2**

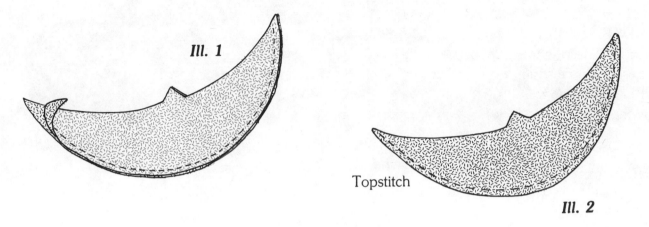

Ill. 1

Topstitch

Ill. 2

5. Sew the visor to the crown, matching the notch to a seam on the crown. **Ill. 3**
6. Fold the visor up.
7. *Bias tape finish:* Open and fold 1" to the wrong side.
8. Place the bias tape right sides together to the bottom of the hat. **Ill. 4**
9. Stitch on the bottom folded line of the bias tape. Overlap the last 1" and cut off the excess tape.
10. Fold the bias tape to the inside. Handstitch or machine stitch the tape around the bottom of the hat.

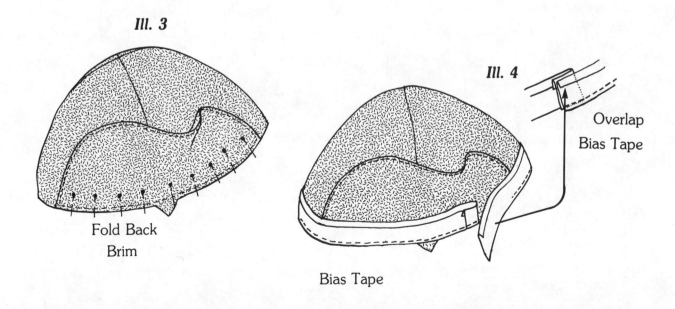

Ill. 3

Fold Back Brim

Ill. 4

Overlap Bias Tape

Bias Tape

8. Calico Chickee

Calico Chickee Materials:

¼ yd. calico (enough fabric for 4 chickees)
Eyes - 2 buttons for each chickee
Beak - orange felt
Wings - ⅔ yd. rickrack for each chickee
Fiberfill stuffing
1 small artificial flower
1-16" narrow ribbon

To make one chickee:

1. Fold the fabric right sides together. Cut a chickee and 2 wings.
2. Edgestitch rickrack around the right side edges of 2 wings.
3. Place the 2 pairs of wings right sides together, and stitch around the outside edge, leaving an opening for turning. *Ill. 1*
4. Turn and stuff lightly. Pin in the raw edges.
5. Machine stitch through all thicknesses on the dashed lines. *Ill. 2*

Ill. 1

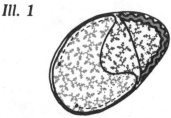

Leave Open

Topstitching

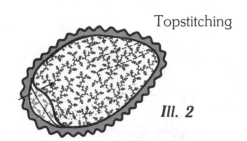

Ill. 2

6. Pin the wing in place on the body. Sew it to the body and close the opening with the same stitching. *Ill. 3*
7. Sew on the button eyes.

Ill. 3

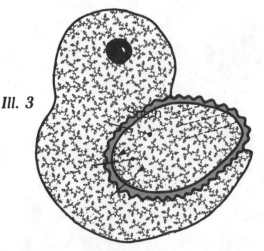

8. Place the two bodies right sides together, and stitch around the outside edge, leaving an opening for turning at the bottom. **Ill. 4**
9. Turn. Stuff. Slipstitch the opening shut.

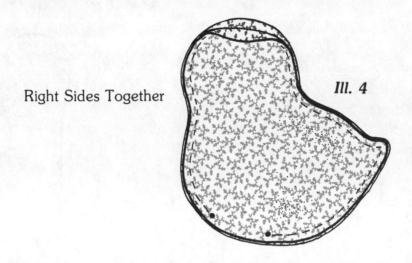

Right Sides Together   **Ill. 4**

10. Cut a beak from orange felt. Fold the beak in half and edgestitch a tuck. **Ill. 5**
11. Refold and handstitch in place. **Ill. 6**
12. Tie a bow around the chickee's neck. Hand-tack on a flower.

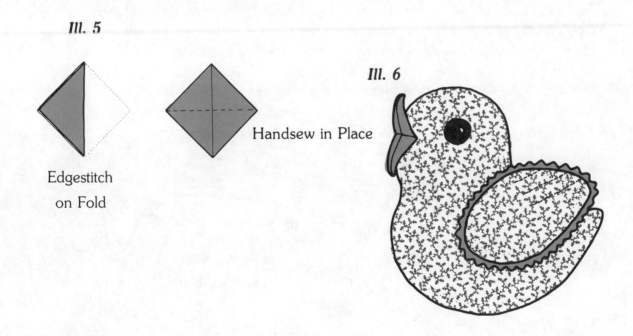

Ill. 5

Edgestitch
on Fold

Ill. 6

Handsew in Place

9. Baseball Glove 'Tooth Fairy' Pillow

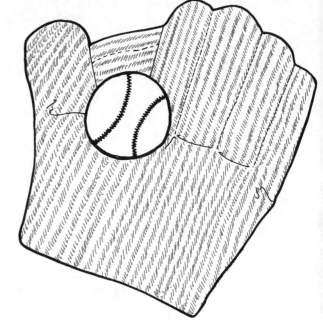

Note to enclose in baseball pocket:
Put your tooth
Behind the ball
Until the tooth fairy
Comes to call.

Baseball Glove - Tooth Fairy Pillow Materials:

⅓ yd. brown or tan corduroy (enough fabric for two)
½ lb. fiberfill stuffing
3" × 5" piece of polyester interfacing or bonded batting
White felt

Web
1. Fold the fabric right sides together. Cut 1 web from the double layer of fabric. Cut 1 from interfacing.
2. Pin the two layers of fabric right sides together. Pin the interfacing on the back side. *Ill. 1*
3. Stitch the long sides. Turn. Topstitch on the long dashed lines. *Ill. 2*

Ill. 1

Batting

Ill. 2

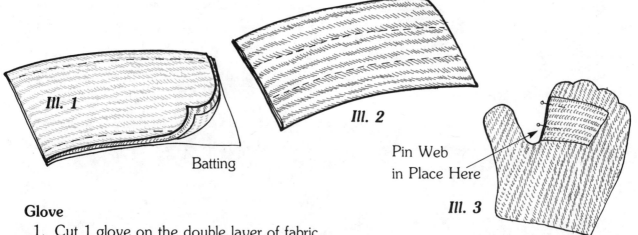

Pin Web in Place Here

Ill. 3

Glove
1. Cut 1 glove on the double layer of fabric.
2. Place the two pieces right sides together, with the web pinned inside and going toward the center of the glove. *Ill. 3*

3. Stitch around the outside edge, leaving the marked space on the thumb and the glove bottom open. *Ill. 4*
4. Clip in at the corners and finger indentations.
5. Turn the glove right side out. Slip the web into place inside the thumb. Fold the bottom of the glove up to the inside web in the thumb, and machine stitch from the inside. *Ill. 5*

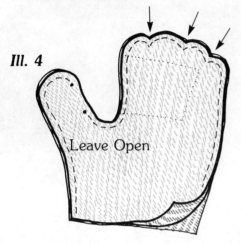

Ill. 4

Leave Open

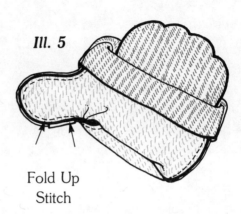

Ill. 5

Fold Up
Stitch

6. Topstitch the *fingers* along the dashed lines. Stuff firmly.
7. Stuff the bottom lightly. Turn the raw edges under on the bottom and edgestitch. *Ill. 6*

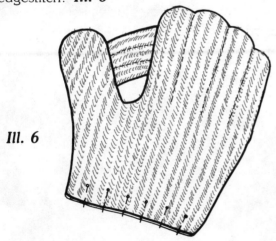

Ill. 6

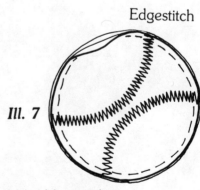

Edgestitch

Ill. 7

Ball
1. Cut 2 from white felt.
2. Machine satin stitch on the dashed line, or draw on the dashed line with a permanent marker. *Ill. 7*
3. Place the two pieces of felt together, with the stitching on the top. Sew part way around the ball. Stuff the ball lightly. Continue sewing around the ball.
4. Whipstitch the bottom half of the stuffed ball to the glove to form a pocket.
5. Write the message and tuck it in the pocket.

10. Rainbow Placemats

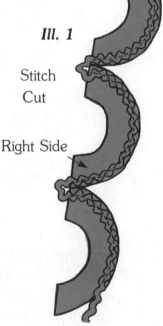

Rainbow Placements - Set of Four Materials:

Rainbow - ¼ yd. pieces of solid yellow, solid orange

⅓ yd. solid blue and solid red

Cloud - ½ yd. white eyelet yardage

1 yd. polyester fleece interfacing

1 yd. backing fabric (may be one of the solid colors)

3 pkgs. wide white rickrack

1 pkg. each of wide rickrack in yellow, red, orange, and blue

1. Rainbow: Cut out all 4 parts of the rainbow and the cloud.
2. Match the rickrack with the solid color. Edgestitch the rickrack along the top of each. Outline the cloud completely.
    Speed Sew Method: Do not cut individual pieces of rickrack. Butt rainbow pieces onto the long piece of rickrack. Cut. ***Ill. 1***

Ill. 1

Stitch

Cut

Right Side

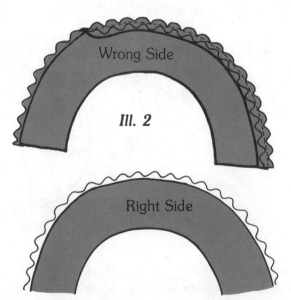

3. Press the rickrack under so that only half of the rickrack shows. Do not press the rickrack under on the solid blue or the sides and bottom of the cloud. ***Ill. 2***

4. Lay out and pin the rainbow on the polyester interfacing. Overlap so that no raw edges show.

5. *Stitch in the ditch* on all rickrack lines. Do not stitch down the outside edges. (the top of the rainbow and the sides and bottom on the cloud) *Ill. 3*

6. Trim the excess polyester fleece away.

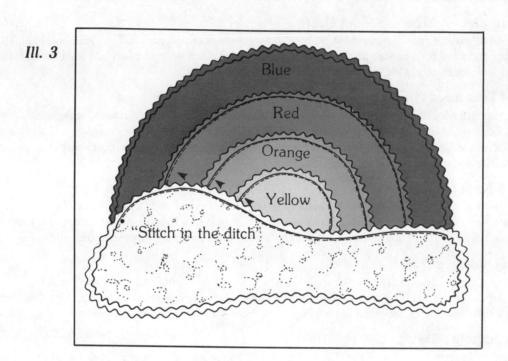

Ill. 3

Blue

Red

Orange

Yellow

"Stitch in the ditch"

7. Place the rainbow on the backing fabric with right sides together. Cut and stitch the backing to the rainbow. Leave an opening for turning. Clip at the corners. *Ill. 4*

8. Turn. Press. Slipstitch the opening shut.

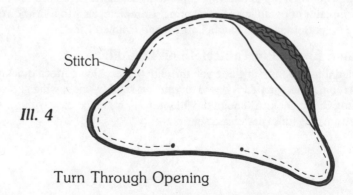

Stitch

Ill. 4

Turn Through Opening

BOOK ORDER INFORMATION

If you do not have a fine quilting shop in your area, you may purchase these products from Quilt in a Day™. Please write for a current price list of the books and quilting supplies available. All of Eleanor's books feature full color cover photographs and numerous detailed illustrations. Many include related pattern variations and projects.

#1001 Quilt in a Day (Log Cabin)

Make a beautiful log cabin quilt in 10-16 hours using the speed-sew techniques in this 88 page book. Concise, step-by-step directions with detailed illustrations are presented so even the beginner can find success.

#1002 The Sampler - A Machine Sewn Quilt

Complete, detailed directions and illustrations show how to speed-sew a sampler quilt. The Quilt is assembled using calicos, laces and trims for a nostalgic touch. All 50 patterns are machine quilted on bonded batting for a soft, dimensional look. Instructions for smaller projects are also given.

#1003 Trio of Treasured Quilts

Three different patterns: Monkey Wrench, Ohio Star and Bear's Paw are featured with quick, complete machine sewing methods. Make one block or a whole quilt using the convenient detailed yardage and cutting charts, as well as Eleanor Burns' assembly-line sewing techniques. This book includes projects easy enough for beginners, yet exciting enough for experienced quilters.

#1004 Lover's Knot Quilt

The ease of Eleanor Burns' assembly-line sewing techniques continues in the Lover's Knot book. This traditional pattern, resembling the intertwining of two wedding bands, is quick to sew and requires only four colors. Additional features of the book include a sawtooth finished edge and a simple to sew dust ruffle.

#1005 Amish Quilt in a Day

The versatile pattern of the "Roman Stripe" goes together easily with strip sewing and quick cutting of the blocks with a rotary cutter. Full color photographs provide examples of many pattern variations. Also described is a unique "quick-turn" method of showing the backing on the front side and mitering the corners.

#1006 Irish Chain in a Day

Quick strip sewing and rotary cutting is all the "Luck of the Irish" you will need to put this quilt together in only a matter of hours. Perfect for a child's first quilt and beginners of all ages, the Single Irish Chain is a joy to create. Experienced sewers will enjoy the more elaborate pattern variation with the Double Irish Chain.

#1009 May Basket Quilt

Yes, even this delightful traditional pattern has not escaped the assembly-line sewing methods of Eleanor Burns. Color it Amish in dark solids or Victorian in light calicos and lace. Even the basket handle is made easy with a quick marking, sewing and pressing technique. Instructions for pillows, shams, and wallhangings included.

#1010 Schoolhouse Wallhanging

Easy strip piecing and assembly-line sewing come together again in the production of this traditional favorite. Absolutely no templates or complicated measuring. Complete, easy to follow directions include four layout variations: Americana Border, Star, Single Lattice, and Framed Block.

#1011 Diamond Log Cabin Tablecloth or Treeskirt

Complete detailed illustrations will guide you through this exciting pattern quickly and the results are sure to brighten up any room. Construction is based on quick assembly-line sewing and strip piecing methods from the Quilt in a Day Log Cabin book. Although the "diamonds" are made easy with rotary cutting on a 60° angle, this project is most rewarding for experienced sewers.

#1012 Morning Star Quilt
In this beautiful traditional design for experienced sewers, an eight pointed star alternates with a chain block. Eleanor explains how to make it via all the quick piecing and assembly techniques that have brought her such renown among quilters.

#1013 Trip Around the World Quilt
Discover the magic of "tubing" and then "unsewing" strips in this perfect beginner book. It is enchanting tied, or for more challenge, it is a fun machine or hand quilted project. Included are instructions on the overlock sewing machine for even quicker quilts.

#1014 Friendship Quilt
The Friendship Quilt book commemorates Quilt in a Day's Tenth Anniversary with the Album Block featured. In addition to Eleanor's easy-to-understand strip piecing instructions, suggestions are given to help you design and assemble your own special Friendship Quilt.

#1015 Dresden Plate Quilt, a Simplified Method, by Wendy Gilbert
This classic Dresden Plate quilt book is packed with easy to understand and clearly illustrated steps for machine sewing the plates and blocks together, strip piecing a lattice and 9-patch border. Included is the invisible applique technique by machine.

#1016 Pineapple Quilt, a Piece of Cake, by Loretta Smith
This traditionally difficult pattern is redrafted for a contemporary look and made easier with modern tools and techniques. For the experienced quiltmaker, it is complete with choice of quilt sizes, yardage charts and easy to follow illustrations and directions. Color photographs inspire an adventure with this Pineapple.

#1017 Radiant Star Quilt
From a variety of sizes, choose a quilt or wallhanging in four or six fabrics. Filled with fabric selection advice, quick sew techniques, and optional finishes, this heavenly book will be enjoyed by the experienced sewer.

#1018 Blazing Star Tablecloth
Turn strips into diamonds and diamonds into a 60" octagonal shaped accent size tablecloth. Detailed instructions for both conventional and serger sewing machines. For the quilt maker with experience.

#1019 Heart's Delight, Nine-Patch Variation, by Patricia Knoechel
Anyone in love with Nine-Patches or Hearts will thrill to the five easy projects of four small quilts and a wreath. Choose from diagonal or straight blocks, planned or scrap fabrics, wallhangings or small quilts!

#1020 Tulip Quilt
Enjoy the freshness of spring tulips all year round. Fast assembly-line sewing methods and a choice of quilt sizes and two block settings will make you want to fill your home with a garden variety of beautiful Tulip Quilts. Recommended for the intermediate sewer.

#1030 Creating With Color, by Patricia Knoechel
Written by a former art teacher, this book explains the basic concepts of combining colors in fabrics and designs so that your next quilting project will be a smashing success. Featuring fan quilts and a fan vest, seven additional patterns are taught, plus many small projects.

Additional Patterns and Projects

#1007 Country Christmas
Sew ten festive decorations with complete full sized patterns and step-by-step directions.

#1008 Bunnies and Blossoms
This delightful book contains full sized patterns and detailed directions for ten quick sewing projects, featuring sock bunnies and their clothes.

#2001 Patchwork Santa, by LuAnn Stout

Enjoy this 30" stuffed Santa as a holiday decoration or child's toy. Included in the book are full size pattern pieces, optional patchwork construction and choice of faces.

#2002 Last Minute Gifts

Choose from an exciting array of nine projects made easily and quickly from simple instructions. Anyone can expect success in the making, joy in the giving.

#2011 Dresden Placemats

Combine quaint calicos and rickrack or lace for these easy country table decorations. Clear illustrations show how to speed cut and sew 16 wedges together into placemats, pillows and a tea cozy.

2012 Angel of Antiquity

A Victorian angel with a rose in her hair and a doily for her halo, she's perfect for the top of any Christmas tree.

#2015 Log Cabin Wreath

The log cabin wreath is an easy to construct, assembly-line sewn wallhanging. The pattern uses light and dark fabrics to create a wreath which becomes an impressive looking beginner's project.

#2016 Log Cabin Christmas Tree

Perfect for the holidays, this wallhanging can be made in a twinkling. Utilizing assembly-line sewing methods, you will find this a delightful project to warm the Christmas spirit in your home.

#2017 Easy Radiant Star Wallhanging

Amazingly simple due to rotary cutting and strip piecing, this giant star will measure 40" x 40" in just six hours!

#2020 Flying Geese Quilt

Capture the beauty and symmetry of wild geese in flight. This seemingly intricate pattern is made easy thanks to Eleanor Burns' quick-sew methods.

Video Tapes

Take Eleanor home with you! You can replay her at each step of quilt making as many times as you need in the comfort and convenience of your own home. Her enthusiasm is contagious! Available in VHS: Quilt in a Day Log Cabin, Monkey Wrench, Ohio Star, Bear's Paw, Lover's Knot, Amish Quilt, Irish Chain, May Basket, Schoolhouse Wallhanging, Diamond Log Cabin, Morning Star, Trip Around the World, Friendship Quilt, Country Christmas, Log Cabin Christmas Tree and Wreath, and Block Party Series 1 and 2. Check on new titles and current pricing. Encourage your local public library to carry Quilt in a Day™ video tapes.

Supplies

Quilt in a Day™ carries a line of essential supplies for creating professional looking quilts, including: rotary cutters and replacement blades, cutting mats with grids, 6" x 6" mini rulers, 6" x 12" and 6" x 24" rulers, and the 12 1/2" x 12 1/2" Square Up. Also available are quilter's pins, magnetic pin holders, magnetic seam guides, curved needles, invisible thread and bicycle clips.

Call or write Quilt in a Day™

1955 Diamond Street, San Marcos, California 92069 For Information Call (619)591-0081

Orders Only Call 1-800- U2 KWILT (1-800-825-9458) Ask for the Mail Order Department